No part of this book may be reproduced or transmitted in any form or by any means, electronic or mechanical, including photocopying, recording, or stored in a retrieval system or otherwise, without the written permission from the publisher. For information regarding permission, write to Kia Harris, LLC, 88 Route 17M, STE 1012, Harriman, NY 10926.

ISBN 978-1-7342186-0-2

Text and illustrations copyright © 2020 by Sarah A. Faison. All rights reserved.
Published by KH Publishers an imprint of Kia Harris, LLC.

The publisher does not have any control over and does not assume any responsibility for author or third-party websites or their content or any other media, social or others.

Printed in the U.S.A.

First Paperback Edition, June 2020

Welcome My Love

Oh, how we anticipate your arrival!

Written by   Sarah A. Faison

Illustrated by   P. Toba Olatunji

ABOUT THE BOOK

Welcome My Love is an inspirational book that is perfect for expectant mothers and families to read aloud to precious little ones while in the womb to familiarize them with the voices of their loved ones and to enhance the bonding experience.

Around week 25 of pregnancy, ears are rapidly developing, and a baby can recognize their mother's voice. Reading loving, soothing, and welcoming words stimulates an interest in sounds. Also, it helps with the development of listening skills while helping to prepare little ones for their birth passage. It's never too early to start telling your baby how loved they are.

Welcome My Love is an excellent book to gift for baby showers, baby sprinkles, baby announcements, gender reveals, baby baptisms, and more. Also, Welcome My Love is perfect for pairing with Bibs Plus baby bibs, blankets, onesies, and other offerings. It celebrates the joy of new life while laying the earliest foundation for a little one's literacy.

Dedication

To all the beautiful unborn babies transitioning to join us, we welcome you. You are God's Masterpieces.

To my husband Fred, I thank you for being my best friend.

To my daughter Jessica, you are my most precious gift.

To my parents Walter and Ida James and brother Greg Swann who I miss so much!

Special Acknowledgements

To my siblings (Linda, Brenda, Mary, Walter Jr., and Priscilla) for your love and support. Glad that we are family.

Andrea Babilya - for your friendship and editing skills.

Erika McClure - for narrating Welcome My Love.

Thank you to my amazing niece Nefray Searight for being the source of artistic inspiration for my book cover.

Welcome my love.

It is beautiful news that you are on your way.

We are so excited about your special day!

Welcome my love.

You are a blessing sent from Heaven to Earth.

How awesome is the miracle of birth.

A precious and perfect gift sent from above.

You are a reflection of love.

Welcome my love.
Awaiting your arrival has brought us healing.

There are simply no words to describe how we're feeling.

Many are looking forward to your gentle touch.

The blessing of your presence will mean so much.

Welcome my love.

Your smile will be like a work of art.
A touch of your hands will soften hearts.

God has entrusted you into our hands.
You are a part of his master plan.

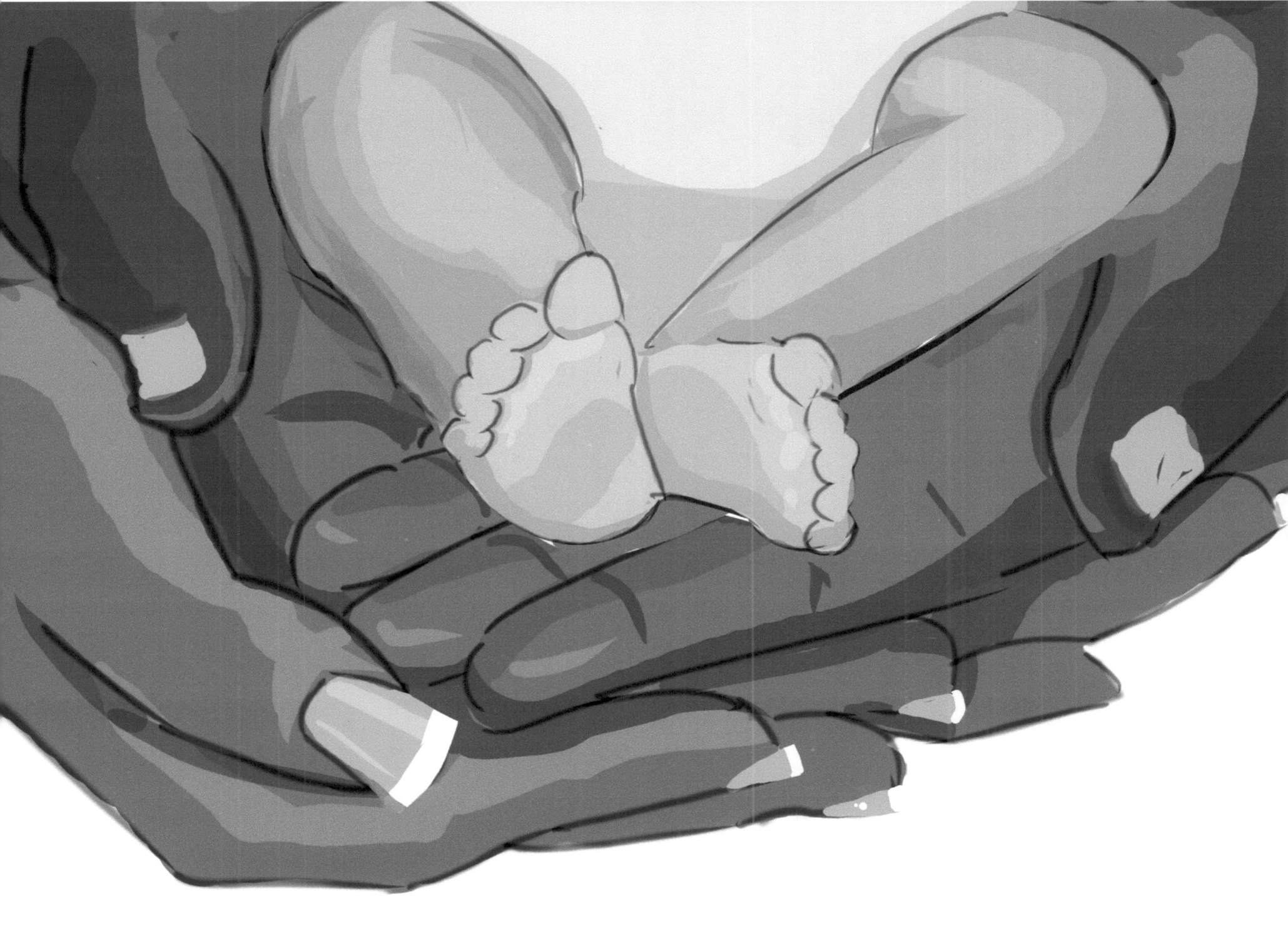

Welcome my love.
Your birth is near.

See you soon my love.

You are beautiful.

"...for I am fearfully
and wonderfully made..."
-Psalms 139:14

"Welcome My Love is a phenomenal story of mother and child and how God knits this amazing gift into the womb and heart of mothers - this child is fearfully and wonderfully made! Hello WORLD here comes a beautiful miracle of life!!"

— Dr. Mary Searight

"Welcome My Love is a beautiful book for expectant mothers to read and bond with their child. Studies confirm the unborn babies can hear sounds while still in the womb. This wonderful story of hope, anticipation, and love reminds us of the power of communication and its power to bring mother and child closer while speaking love into the world. What a wonderful way to prepare for a new life! The perfect book for an expectant mother."

— Gina Marcello, Ph.D.

Positive affirmations are powerful brief statements designed to encourage positive thoughts, attitudes, and happy feelings. They are based on widely accepted and well-established psychological theory.

A key benefit of self-affirmation is reduced stress. I have created a link to my YouTube Channel of positive affirmations for expectant moms. Feel free to enjoy.

bit.ly/MomandBabyBondingAffirmations

www.ingramcontent.com/pod-product-compliance
Lightning Source LLC
Chambersburg PA
CBHW041819080526

44587CB00005B/147